THE WAYS IN WHICH WE ARE LIKE BIRDS

COLLECTED POEMS

ELISABETH PIKE

ABOUT THE AUTHOR

Elisabeth Pike writes fiction and poetry. Her debut novel *Murmuration* was shortlisted for the Kindle Storyteller Award 2024. She lives in Shropshire. Find her at elisabethpike.co.uk.

Copyright 2025 by Elisabeth Pike.

All right reserved.

This edition first published March 2025 by Little Bird Editions.

No part of this book may be reproduced in any form or by any electronic or mechanical means, including information storage and retrieval systems, without written permission from the author, except for the use of brief quotations in a book review.

CONTENTS

HOMING
From *September,* 2008

UNCLE JOHN
    NY
    Decay
    Little Wooden Chair
    Phone Call
    Ode to Reading Station
    Rain
    Rio
    Even Still

NESTING
From *There You Are,* 2017

. . .

SNOW
- Afterwards
- How Terrifying
- Darkness
- There You Are
- Love Poem
- Scan
- Laundry
- Something in Between
- Pied Piper
- A Walk Near Shere
- Waiting for Ivy
- Lemon Cake
- Moment
- Guildford
- Si Paloma
- Crying in Public Places
- My Boy, My Girl
- Spring Nights
- December
- Charterhouse
- July Thunder
- Little Park
- Trembling Heart
- Type 1
- Thunderstorm
- Half Past Nine
- The Bells
- Kind
- Kiss on the Lips
- Little Car
- Nap
- Five Thirty

Sand Martins
Inwood

MIGRATION

Petals
    On Leaving a Place
    Weight
    Freefall
    Dittisham
    Sadness
    Longing
    Cardigan
    Younger, Happier
    Uncoupling
    Raye
    Animae

THERE WE WERE (from *Paper Birds*)

SONG

FROM *VOICE AT THE WINDOW*, **One Hundred Poems of Gratitude written during lockdown, 2020**

GRATITUDE # 6
    Gratitude # 7

Gratitude # 19
Gratitude # 25
Gratitude # 43
Gratitude # 49
Gratitude # 52
Gratitude # 57
Gratitude # 59
Gratitude # 70
Gratitude # 71
Gratitude # 77
Gratitude # 82
A Note to the Creatives
Gratitude #85
Gratitude #87
Gratitude #92
Gratitude #95
Gratitude #106
Gratitude #113
Gratitude #115
Gratitude #120
Gratitude # 130
Gratitude #133
Gratitude # 147
Gratitude #154
Gratitude #166
Gratitude #181

PREENING

SOMETIMES
    Sometimes it Feels Impossible

The Ways in Which We Are Like Birds

Ash
Seed Pods
Mouthful
Curled Like a Cat
Like a Whip
Ukraine
Magnolia
Piano
Swallow
Half Marathon
Sleep
Hope
At Whixall Moss
Alliums
Ridge Line
Soak
Dreamer's Workshop
Mexican Wave
Bluebell

From Lent Poems

CLEANSE
    See
    Walk
    Follow
    Promise
    Room
    For Sarah
    Keep Watch
    Sacrifice

Cross
Cloths
Hidden
Darkness
Wait
Dawn

FLIGHT

I AM Woman
    Love
    On Hearing
    Clearing, Spring
    Bones
    Mother
    Yearlet
    Having a Hard Time
    Maple
    Sometimes
    Things the Summer Teaches
    Rose
    Unfurl
    Speak, River-Sea
    Why Does It Take So Long?

HOMING
FROM SEPTEMBER, 2008

Uncle John

The jam, thick with whole strawberries,
    hadn't seemed so wonderful to me at the time.
    Only now, sitting in my room with morning toast,
    do I feel the loss,
    as I remember them sliding out of the jar
    on to the newly buttered toast.

My eyes would be wide with the breakfast spread,
    hidden all night under the rust-coloured cloth,
    which was whipped off come morning,
    to pour fresh tea into teacups,
    that had been upturned through the night,
    to stand the loaf on its end and slice the top off
    as though it were a ham.

. . .

THE HOUSE WAS FALLING DOWN, they said,
    was bulldozed, in the end, for level bricks and double-glazing.
    Even the garden is now straight and neatly pruned,
    and the plot looks smaller, much smaller, when empty.

BUT I STILL SEE THE tall grass and the apple trees,
    I still feel the scratch of the rusty barrel under my feet
    as I roll it across the lawn,
    I see the sheds collapsed
    around the piles of junk inside them.

THERE WAS a face that we chalked on the wall with my uncle.
    We would pretend it was our headmaster and hurl apples at it,
    watching them smash against his chalk cheek
    and dribble down his brick neck.

IN THE YEARS after John's death it faded,
    and each passing summer we would retrace it,
    to try to etch it into permanence,
    until one year we couldn't find its outline
    and didn't know where to start.

WE, so young, so unknowing,
    had probably forgotten or moved on faster -

because we had energy, and less memories.

And eventually it was normal for him to not be there anymore,

but not for his mother, or my father.

He had no children to carry on
his laugh,
his genes,
his foolishness.

NY

'Tipped out toy box of a place,' she said,
    and I thought she must have been there
    because that is just what I thought when I went there too.
    In the hostel, the white pipes clanked all night,
    and there was the smell of stale smoke along the corridor.
    It felt surreal to be there, the place so steeped in history,
    so walked upon, so described.
    The streets were loud with voices
    clamouring to be heard outside the window.
    We took the train up to Beacon and on the way
    the Hudson was wide and choppy,
    it bit against the shore and slapped against the rocks.
    We watched from the window
    as we wheeled around the edge of the shore,
    the water went right under the lines.
    On the last day, we walked from the Met back to the hostel
    and the rain drenched us to the bone.
    We changed down to our underwear
    and then went to catch our flight.
    Arriving back home in England,
    we unfurled the clothes that had been rolled
    tightly in the bag, dripping New York rain
    onto the carpet.

Decay

Now that I think about it, it was all about decay.
    The car was left for years in the garage;
    It's fold-down cup holders, the most glamorous novelty.
    We would climb in and pretend that we were going
    on holiday, drinking lemonade.

There is a picture of me ruddy-cheeked,
    held in place on a tractor that was sunken into the mud
    and had not been anywhere in years.
    My mother tells me a tractor grumbled into life not far from us,
    and I thought we had started ours, inadvertently,
    and would be rushed away without knowing
    how we'd started it, or how to stop it.

There was the mildewed caravan
    that Uncle John pretended was his home.
    It was filled with elastic bands
    and rolls of cellophane.
    Everything had a slightly surreal air,
    as if it was all made up.

Like that time Santa walked past the window,
    And then John came down from his shower, claiming innocence.
    I thought there was something fishy going on,
    but he had wet hair, and I couldn't be sure.

Little Wooden Chair

I DIDN'T USED to trust you,
    when you first appeared in my house -
    he found you in a skip, you see.
    I put you in the corner
    and ignored you, I never once sat on you.

NOW THOUGH, you are part of the family –
    tucked under the table with the others.
    See how my cardigan droops
    affectionately over you!

Phone Call

The phone rang long distance from Beijing
    just as the turkey was being carved.
    At first it was all squeals and hellos,
    before they went back to eating,
    wearing their lopsided cracker hats like fools.
    But I sat there behind the curtain, talking with you.
    We used up your whole phonecard,
    pretending that we'd been together at Christmas.
    You didn't want to talk much about what you had done that day,
    and me either, for fear it would have made you cry.
    So we skirted around the conversation and
    I was distracted by the falling snow outside the window.

When I sat back down to eat, everyone else had finished theirs.
    My plated meal had turned cold, but it didn't matter
    that I shovelled it down, lukewarm,
    or that I missed the feast that comes only once a year,
    Because I had your voice on the line,
    younger sister, from the other end of the planet.
    and that was more to me than Christmas.

Ode to Reading Station

I HAD NEVER KNOWN what to associate with the name
    all the way through my youth:
    it had always been one of those smoky places,
    dull, grey and nothing more.
    But ever since I went to uni,
    it was the place that held hands with you and me.
    It was the thing that came up between us,
    that we had a fondness for each time we passed through
    (it meant we were half-way there).

STANDING HERE in the cold morning it feels good
    to be on my way to you, to the South West.
    It smells of diesel and the engines are loud.
    The rain falls like silver wires between the two platforms
    and strikes me as quite beautiful
    (but perhaps this is because I am on my way to you
    and nothing more).

Rain

I JUST DROVE through the most incredible traffic
    to get here, back home.
    It had been raining through the night,
    but I didn't think of that, as I left my house to go shopping,
    and it was only as I was driving down Ladymead,
    with the scores of other cars,
    that I realised I wasn't going to get anywhere fast.

THE DROPS WERE PELTING down with such force
    that they leapt back up from the bonnets and metal roofs.
    I thought it was funny, all these people ignoring nature -
    when the sensible thing would have been to stay inside,
    out of the rain.

AND NOW, back inside my dry room
    I wonder why I am not elsewhere,
    and why I can still hear the hum of motors
    above the fall of rain
    through the open window.

Rio

I WAS PROBABLY ABOUT ten years old.

I had named the Russian hamster Rio after the car I wanted.

It was too shy to play with me though,

and I would chase it around its cage to try to pick it up.

One day it escaped, and I scoured the whole house looking for it.

I shut the cat in a room to keep her out of the way.

And it was only after hours of searching that I thought

what if the hamster and the cat are in the same room?

They were, and Rio's tail had been stripped of its skin,

but he was still alive, and I put him back in his cage.

A FEW DAYS later he died from the stress of it.

I took him to church with me in a shoebox

to try to come to terms with it,

my mum said it would be a good idea.

On the way there, I reached inside the box and held him.

His body still felt warm, and I cried 'He's alive!'

but she looked at me doubtfully,

and I realised it was just the pulse of my thumb against his fur.

Even Still

As when
>   it seems that there is nothing left,
>   nothing but a shred of yourself.
>   Like a flag on a hilltop,
>   bare and waiting.

As when the wind comes rushing through,
>   with the train going by
>   at the station,
>   the hot fumes pushed
>   into your face like a bad kiss:
>   a dirty kick from life that says
>   even though.
>   Even though you do all of this;
>   you stand here on this
>   dull, grey platform,
>   and you jostle amongst the
>   elbows and shoulders of strangers.
>   Even though your mouth tastes of strong coffee
>   and you have not quite woken fully,
>   and your mind is thinking back to last night,
>   to those words that you said.

Even though, you will come
>   from your shell, your carapace today;
>   you will be pushed out of hiding by this life.
>   That thing that you carry,
>   your burden, your heart-shaped weight

will come out and show itself,
shy and beautiful pearl
that it is, or might be,
given half a chance.

NO MATTER HOW YOU FEEL,
    it is rising.

THERE IS NO APOLOGY:
    you will be blown through,
    turned inside out like glass,
    molten, taking shape,
    or a lump of dough in the bakers' hands,
    kneaded until ready,
    broken until supple,
    like a flag in the wind,
    ragged and waiting.

IT WILL NOT BE CRUSHED
    by this sometimes hard and cruel life,
    a smouldering wick will not be snuffed out,
    but the faint spark of grace will come,
    and what you have
    will be galvanised in your hands.

FOR THERE, hidden behind weary eyes,
    beyond the drudge of work,
    and the weight of worry
    is a bright light.

The Ways in Which We Are Like Birds

. . .

AND IT WILL COME THROUGH, even still,
    as the player in the pit
    tightens his reed in place,
    presses his lips to the mouthpiece and blows,
    and the clear note comes through
    as you never thought it might,
    from two inches of reed,
    and a piece
    of black wood.

NESTING

FROM THERE YOU ARE, 2017

Snow

We were at a friends' house the night before
and opened the door to the flurry of snowflakes.
We drove home slowly with the windows open;
it was cold and the snow fell in spirals.
It was unlike anything we'd seen, even then,
and in the morning, we woke, breath-held to see it
white and deep, like a dream.
The phone call came saying that the school was closed and
we got dressed and ran out into the street.
It was so quiet that it seemed no one else had even woken.
We were as excited as schoolchildren,
running to Jen's at eight in the morning
because we didn't know what else to do.

The Ways in Which We Are Like Birds

. . .

We walked around the streets,
    took a tray up to the Downs and made tracks in it.
    Came home and took all our clothes off and went to bed.
    Funny to think that that's where you began,
    that out of joy you were sown,
    little bird settling under the snow.

Afterwards

In the bath, I hear the faint tap
    of rain against the window.
      I open it and lie back and listen.

I am different now, than I have ever been.
    Nothing will ever be the same
    for another person has come from me;
    I am forever split in two.

I am no longer just me,
    just here -
    listening to the rain fall,
    the way I always used to,

for half of me is elsewhere.

How Terrifying

How terrifying, that night we first brought you home!
    I did not trust your lungs to work by themselves
    and I reached over in the dark to you,
    to feel for your nose and lips,
    to make sure you weren't smothered.

You would snuffle and grunt
    and I would move my hand
    and lie there in the pitch dark,
    my body turned to you,
    guardian, watcher of your little soul.

I chased away my sleep with worry
    as I listened for your breaths,
    feeling like the only one in the world
    who could hear you,
    who was listening out for you.

Darkness

In the darkness of night, I lie between the two of you
    and check that I can single you out.
    One by one your breaths fall like stars in the dark.

There You Are

There you are,
    little pulse of life.
    Your slow breaths
    come crackling through
    on the monitor.
    I lift it to my ear
    every now and then
    and hear the static
    and press it closer
    to hear you there.

I think of the first scan we had,
    when we saw you
    wriggling away,
    your spine a lit-up fish.
    You had so much room then,
    so much energy,
    and swam around,
    unaware that we were watching,
    already delighting in you.

Love Poem

I LOVE him in the bath tonight.
    He is sitting in front of me,
    and the bones of his shoulder blades
    jut out like little wings beneath his pale skin.
    I'm humbled with it all again
    which I haven't felt in so long,
    the tears and the tiredness having got in the way.

BUT HERE IT IS AGAIN,
    the flash of wonder at you, for being just you,
    for having grown in me, all by yourself.
    for knowing when to be born.
    for being here now, all smiles and squawks.

I RUN my finger down your soapy back
    and remember how it looked on the scan, little fish.

AND I REMEMBER that I fell in love with your father
    for the silly things like that:
    the shoulder blades,
    the shape of his toes,
    the sound of his laugh.

Scan

The lady in the ultrasound room says,
    'Oh look at its little feet! It's being very well behaved,'
    and I think this is someone who is just doing her job
    and yet she acts as if I am important.
    Here she is loving my baby, a perfect stranger to her.
    And there you are.
    It's astounding how alive, how at home you are.
    Like nothing we know, nothing we can remember.
    Eleven-month-old Sam laughs
    as I lie on the bench with my tummy out.
    He doesn't understand as we tell him
    that there is his baby sister on the screen.
    He just laughs at the box of blue rubber gloves,
    his face in the mirror, the lights in the ceiling,
    wondering at things all the while.

Laundry

I STAND out amongst the whites in the yard,
    still hung up to dry though it is getting dark.
    I gather them in, the stone slabs
    rough and warm beneath my feet.

A HUNDRED VOICES hum and a few doors slam
    at the close of day in this town.
    Yellow kitchen light spills across the car park
    where the boys from up the road do tricks on their skateboards.
    The scrape of their wheels on the tarmac
    etches itself into my remembering.

FLOTSAM NUDGES up to each back door
    leaving unwanted tidelines.
    Things heard around here cannot be unheard.
    Everyone knows what goes on, but still,
    when they wake, in the cold morning light,
    they prowl around the edges of their property,
    guarding their lives, their small secrets.

AND I MINE, I suppose,
    for behind this blue gate,
    and beyond this tatty yard,
    within this see-through house,
    as frail as a skeleton,
    are all my life's treasures.

Something in Between

I loved him first for his innocence.
    He gulped full glasses of milk like he was eight,
    he took me out to buy sweets from the corner shop,
    he smelled like clean washing and fresh breath.
    Just being with me made him happy, he said.
    I thought he was making it up.
    I was eighteen and about to go around the world.
    He stood on my doorstep and asked if he could kiss me.

We were living those in between years where the future
    was an unknown treasure, one that was good and only good.
    When I left, he gave me a present; he said to open it on the plane.
    As soon as I had strapped myself in, I rifled through my rucksack to find it.

It was a photo of him as a child sitting on the beach.
    I thought I saw my son there in his young body.
    He had turned to look over his shoulder to the camera,
    and the sun shone down onto his brown back.
    I ran my finger over that small bare arm and wondered
    why it is that young children are so heart-breaking.
    And I flew off to a different country
    knowing for sure that my future lay behind me.

And now we have a son,

and he is not the same as that little boy in the picture.
I look at him and think,
you are neither your father nor your mother,
you are something in between,
something we could never have guessed at,
and that is what makes you beautiful.

Pied Piper

Walking down the high street,
   where the cobbles send my boy to sleep in his pushchair,
   there is a woman playing the hang drum.
   She sits cross-legged on the pavement,
   her clothes bland, layered, tatty,
   her dreads scraped back into a hair band.
   She looks down as she plays.

She curves around the drum
   and her fingers play lightly like raindrops,
   falling and running.
   There are ten instruments at once
   coming from the dome of this drum,
   bronze and dimpled,
   held in the circle of her body.

I walk on,
   and the notes follow me
   like clear perfume
   down this high street,
   that is all shops and business
   until this lightness comes.

It runs after me and
   I am one of the Pied Piper's children,

mesmerised, enchanted.
I turn my head to catch the last strains of it,
as it fades out of hearing.

A Walk Near Shere

'Big, big muddy puddles!' Sam said, over and over
    and he jumped in them until his shoes were wet through.
    Hail fell around us, and the sky had turned dark,
    but it felt good to be outside, even still.

Waiting for Ivy

Waiting for you,
    I could not explain the frustration
    or the melancholy,
    because I knew that you were safe,
    the best kind of safe,
    and that you would come
    when you were ready.
    But it felt like a sorrow in me,
    something that was wrong,
    something that I couldn't fix.
    I missed you, I wanted to know you,
    to touch your face, to hold you.

But now here you are, happily feeding,
    your cool hands spreading and grasping at my skin,
    your wrists no more than two centimetres wide.
    You won't sleep on your own,
    only between us, or on Daddy's chest,
    so, the nights are whispers, cuddles and half-light,
    and we don't mind at all.

Lemon Cake

And the night after the frustrations,
    there is a clarity,
    like the first bite of a lemon cake
    or a gin and tonic, slipped down the neck.
    There is space for the first time in a long time.
    I am hair-washed, sitting in a house clean and dusted,
    the stillness of an orange dusk glowing outside.
    Ivy sleeps by me in the kitchen,
    in the night-time light.
    It is so quiet that all I can hear
    is the click of the timer on the boiler,
    the little husky breaths she takes,
    the rattle of the cat flap as the cat runs in.
    There is nothing else,
    just the darkness of the window in front of me
    where I imagine people might be looking in,
    but I have become used to it, over time,
    this house, this little life.

Moment

A MOMENT to myself
    while they sleep upstairs.
    Conversations from the street outside
    float through the window,
    a plane drones in the sky.
    I listen to the brush of sandpaper
    on a window frame,
    the slam of a car door,
    the call of an unknown bird.
    It is these little things
    that I forget to listen for these days,
    above the delightful clamour
    of two small voices.

Guildford

'Goodit', you both call it,
    and you know it for the big park,
    the playgroups,
    your little friends.
    And it is home to you.
    Even this small house,
    which we are bursting
    from the seams of,
    is home.
    Happy innocence -
    you do not want for anything more
    than everything that we already have.

Si Paloma

The blossom bounces in the breeze,
    so light against the evergreens,
    So full against the bare deciduous
    It hangs like hope, like promise,
    as I sit in my car
    on the garage forecourt,
    waiting for him to get wine
    so we can go to a friend's.

Samuel sleeps in his car seat, and
    we are late, as usual,
    but it doesn't matter
    because the sound of Si Paloma fills the car,
    and for once the sky is as empty and bright as clean glass,
    because we have decided to pick up where we left off,
    to keep on going no matter how tired we are.

Crying in Public Places

This time it is me again,
    in a room of friends,
    a room of strangers.
    At the door of my son's preschool
    when he shouts 'Don't like preschool'
    the whole way there,
    and leaps from the buggy board
    and runs off down the road.
    I hand him over, howling
    and have to turn from him
    and walk out of the door.

Or he is as good as gold
    the whole morning,
    and holds it together
    until he stands there, coat off,
    ready for the day.
    And then he turns to me
    and quietly starts to cry,
    burying his face in my knee.

My Boy, My Girl

My boy, how could I describe him
    if you had not met him?
    He is a deer with his shining blue eyes,
    he is peaceful and fierce in a breath.
    I read his story tonight,
    and he said, 'Go sleep mummy',
    and held my hand,
    and slipped off into his dreams,
    my lion-heart, dove gentle boy.

And my girl, how would you know
    if you had not seen the curl of her eyelashes,
    the silky warmth of her cheek,
    the explosion of her laugh?
    We are shocked and in love with her,
    this faithful warrior,
    bursting with life and passion
    from every seam of herself.

I am happier now, than I ever have been.
    Two babies is what I was made for.

Spring Nights

It was on those light spring nights
    in that tiny terrace, that they danced.
    They would strip to nothing after tea,
    peeling off their t-shirts
    with caked-on mash and beans,
    and twirl around.
    We never knew what to do with them
    for that hour after we had eaten,
    so, we would leave the washing up
    and make hot tea,
    crash onto the sofa and watch
    as they spun, these pearls of light,
    these wonders that had turned up in our lives,
    and consumed us so utterly.

There was wonder in their eyes
    as they tried to get their bodies
    to move how they wanted,
    to get this thing called music
    under their skin.

December

The fairy lights are on and twinkling,
    the children sleep in their bedroom.
    How wonderful, how mundane.
    Yet there is someone who doesn't know,
    who can't feel the bite of this
    winter's air on her cheek,
    who cannot hear the blandness of her children's
    arguments and wish that they were in bed.
    She cannot feel the relief of handed in assignments,
    or know the crunch of a piece of toast smothered in jam.
    I think of you Jo, all the time.
    Sad that you had to go so quickly.
    Angry, still, that you couldn't say goodbye.

CHARTERHOUSE

AND WHAT HAVE I loved the most, this weekend?
    Walking out of the wedding speeches
    to see lovely Charterhouse at dusk,
    where the children ran and ran
    across the cricket green,
    their feet bare upon the wet lawn,
    where the rain fell like mist on our cheeks
    and smudged the last of the light away.

AND THEN TODAY on the blowy beach,
    with the blue-grey clouds on the horizon,
    we buried Sam up to his neck in the sand.
    There was the space, you see,
    to be quiet and to run and run,
    and that is what we most needed.

July Thunder

We were at playgroup,
    the last of term in a heatwave.
    The grass had turned to straw and the children
    ran about in their swimming costumes.
    Then the colour went out from the sky
    and a clap of thunder made us jump.
    The rain fell on us like God was pouring it from a bucket,
    and the children screamed in unison.
    We laughed at the audacity of the weather,
    and picked up the little ones that came running.

Little Park

'Can we go to the little park?'
    they'd ask after dinner
    and we'd make sweet tea and go over there.
    It was quiet in the faded evenings,
    all the other children in their homes, watching TV.
    It was just us then, and our cat
    calling through the fence.

It was the first place we took our three-day old son
    to sunbathe his jaundice away.
    It was my help through the four years living there,
    packed as tight as sardines in that tiny terrace.
    The place where our tree grew, just for us, we said.
    It filled the window of our lounge
    with its shimmering, turning leaves.

Samuel learnt to ride his yellow bike there last summer,
    when we couldn't do anything but wait
    because there was a house sale to go through,
    and another baby coming.

And we were standing there in the sun
    when we got the call to say that we'd got the house, -
    this mysterious 3 Church Road where we live now.

        . . .

It's funny, the way things go,
    the moment things change,
    the way we walk blind into blessings.

Trembling Heart

I HELD you to me on the bed and smelt your hair, felt your lightness
    as your father bustled in the darkness for your favourite things.
    We had been to the doctor's that afternoon, and he rang as we were driving home
    to the clear light, where the town stopped and the hills began.

I SAW the phone number flash up on the screen and thought 'Shit, it's serious'.
    Something far down in me had sensed that it wasn't going to go away,
    but I wasn't prepared to listen to that, wasn't ready to have you here like this,
    breathing against me like a baby bird.

YOUR FATHER HAD BROUGHT you home from the hospital.
    It was late at night, and he had to take you back again.
    His face was white, and he wasn't thinking straight.
    And I held you on the bed thinking this is the last time;
    the last time that you are mine,
    that you do not have diabetes,
    that everything is okay.
    .

I HAD to kiss you goodbye and send you off
    to that white, unforgiving hospital

while I stayed home for the baby,

But I remember holding you on that bed.
    The drum of my heart was loud,
    and I was so small in your arms,
    and all I had left was this helplessness.

Type I

WALKING out of hospital
    on a cold but bright day,
    clutching armfuls of her silly things;
    Mr Carrot and Mr Strawberry,
    her walking ahead of us
    all jolly and light,
    singing even
    in the October dusk,
    and us following behind,
    tearful and uncertain.
    The bag of drugs they give us
    to take home is almost as big as she is
    and I feel more afraid than I did
    when our first-born came home,
    swaddled with blankets and worry,
    as the silver Sharan carried him.

Thunderstorm

We are woken this morning by a rumble of thunder.
    You sit up in our bed at 5am and say
    'I'm not scared of thunderstorms anymore'
    as if it is a perfectly reasonable thing to say at such a time.

Later, there is a break in the rain
    and we walk through the farmer's field behind the house.
    The sky is big and beautiful,
    it stops me in my tracks
    and reminds me of my smallness;
    a good thing to remember sometimes.

Half Past Nine

It is half past nine when we step outside
    into our clear, beautiful garden
    and inhale a lungful each of this sweet night air.
    I pull the washing (still damp) from the line
    and you gather up the faded plastic toys
    that the kids have scattered around.
    We fold up the teepee, look up at the pink sky
    and think this life is good.

The Bells

You should have seen it today,
    a thousand raindrops battering on the tarmac,
    shivering the leaves of the trees,
    drumming their green skin harder and faster.
    I held my Benjamin at the open window,
    his eyes lit with wonder.

You should have heard it tonight, here in our front room,
    the clatter and din of the church bells so loud
    that they seemed to be shouting into the evening sky,
    'Don't go to bed! Joy, joy, joy!'

Kind

There are times like these where the sun is kind in the morning,
    where it kisses your skin with sweetness,
    even your toes, still damp from the morning dew.

I remember it last year, my belly swelling under my clothes,
    the weight of my prayers on my shoulders,
    the sighs in my lungs each morning.

But it was the kindness of the sun that kept me going,
    as our feet wandered their way to the little preschool.

Kiss on the Lips

Sometimes I want it to go on forever,
    the exhaustion that I feel
    this summer evening.
    There is an ache in my belly
    for these little people who need me.
    The thought of them growing up
    is too painful to think about just now,

so let's pretend that
    you will always come and sit on my lap for cuddles,
    give me a kiss on the lips,
    hold my hand as we walk down the street.

Little Car

She whispers to me in her bed, in the half-light.
　　She says 'There's a little car at Grandma's,
　　I'll show you, I'll get it out of the shed.'
　　She is serious, her face set, her eyes shining.
　　I can't remember why she started talking about the car,
　　or what it has to do with the book that we were reading,
　　but it doesn't matter.
　　She is precious, and all of her thought trails
　　and each of her breaths.

Nap

In a blustery playground my boy has fallen asleep,
    and the wind wraps around us like a blanket.
    There is space and time, of a sort,
    and I stand with my hands in my pockets,
    the brook rushing by behind me.
    I hear its eddies and ripples,
    see the winter light brimming and spilling over,
    winding its way through the trees.
    And I wonder, is this what Virginia meant,
    when she talked of dipping your heart
    deep into the stream?

Five Thirty

It is the moments like this
    that make it all worthwhile.
    The five-thirty wake up,
    and then you come outside
    and see the blue-grey mist
    wrap itself around the mountains,
    and you see the light of dawn
    come blazing through, like pure gold.

And even though you have hardly slept,
    here is a moment of heaven touching earth.
    And it is made even more beautiful, perhaps,
    because of how fragile you feel.
    And it is a reminder that there is not just you
    and your smallness here,
    there is something more.

Sand Martins

The sand martins dip and dive
    towards home,
    where their young await them,
    heads peeping.

Across the river,
    we sit with our young tribe
    and think how fast the time has gone,
    and how much they have grown;
    these three beauties that we are in some way
    and in no way responsible for.

We sit quietly,
    watching
    as the brook runs on.

Inwood

They start at the bottom,
    go a little way,
    have us catch them.
    'Again,' they say,
    'A bit higher!'

We sledge at Inwood
    down steep grass banks.
    It lights up their eyes
    just as it surely did for us
    when we were young.
    And I realise that in so many ways
    it is good to come full circle,
    to come back home.

MIGRATION

Petals

THEY WOULD SCATTER LIKE PETALS,
    drop from my back,
    the moment that I left, I knew.
    I would stand up and shake them off,
    noiselessly
    to the ground.
    And there would be new things
    and I would walk
    unfettered
    towards them,
    bare feet on the ground,
    my hand shielding my eyes
    against the sun.

On Leaving a Place

You wonder if you should just snip the thread and go quietly;
    especially when it goes on like this, and you have been holding on for so long.

You are still here but are longing to be elsewhere,
    and you have already said goodbye.

Weight

It is the weight that you take in a place. Or not.

(Sometimes you feel no one would even notice if you were gone.)

Sometimes you feel as slight as a bird,
    and that it would be just as well to go and land somewhere else.

When all you really want is for someone to look at you,
    or the place where you were, to say,

something is missing from here.

Freefall

FLUTTER OF LEAVES, flutter of farewells.
    Today everything is in free fall.
    There is a mountain of papers
    and somewhere beneath the compost,
    the ash, I am coming alive.
    Ben and I watch from the window as a bird darts
    and leaps around the yard.
    He pushes the leaf mulch with his beak
    And pulls a pink worm from it.
    Three times, searching for his prize.

Dittisham

THERE ARE GRAVELLED PATHS, a snail parade across the way,
> blue slate walls and ferns looping over the path.

We walk up and up and turn to see the blue arm of the river,
> freckled with white boats.

> A spring flows down next to the path.

> Everything is still in the afternoon and amber sun.

> Down on the pontoon, a couple of kids lower raw bacon on strings
>> into the water and pull them up again.

> 'I've got six! More than you!' one shrieks to their wriggling cluster of crabs.

> We cannot imagine living in a place so beautiful.

Sadness

It is like a lurch in the heart,
    not a pang of love,
    but that same throb.
    It gathers at the centre of my ribcage,
    a fistful of cloth.
    It is a pebble, hard and smooth
    that will not be moved or chipped away.
    It is a mouth fixed into a resigned stare,
    a gentle sigh that starts like hope and then fades.
    It is my friend, my companion,
    a full stop to my day.
    It is the zip that is closed along my lips.
    It is the red centre, the quiet heart of me.

Longing

You speak to me of longing,
    and it seems a thing I don't yet know.
    I longed for a child, the first,
    I longed for a garden.
    I knew you before I longed for you but
    my daughter and second son were gifts of grace to me.
    I don't long for my writing,
    because I feel that there is time,
    I don't feel rushed and that is a grace.
    But you are unfulfilled,
    because you are not in the land yet, and
    you have been walking for a long time.
    But this longing is a precious thing;
    it is a holy fire,
    it burns away all that is peripheral,
    unneeded.

Cardigan

You will grow up and discard me like
    A worn cardigan,
    full of the smells of garlic and chilli,
    flung onto the washing pile.
    I am the husk from which you bloomed,
    I grew you all carefully,
    unknowingly,
    but now you don't need me.
    You shed me like an old skin,
    And it smarts and it makes me think
    What am I here for then?
    You were my purpose,
    my whole being, and now
    you don't need me anymore.

Younger, Happier

We watch back this video we made of us, younger, happier.

The children have tears in their eyes at how happy we were.

They both say I want to be little again, and we all feel the same.

I want to be little again too, I whisper
    to my cobweb covered ceilings,
      to my flaking windowpanes.

Uncoupling

TWO METAL FISTS

UNCLENCH

AND THE ONE truck slips
    silently
    back
    into the inky night.

THERE IS a stunned silence between us,
    we were not waiting for this.
    How could we have counted the cost
    when we did not see this coming?

WE THOUGHT that we would see home again,
    that things would go back to how they were before,
    but they have not,
    and never will,
    and we know that now.

THERE ARE SECRET LOSSES, perhaps,
    borne by all these women, cloven in two,
    borne by all these men who are unchanged
    but for whom the world has changed.

        · · ·

We used to give up anything for our love,
    it was well-fed and watered,
    but now we say there is not the time.

It never seems there is enough;
    and I think of that truck
    slipping
    silently
    back,

of the men working on the tracks
    who didn't even hear it coming;
    it took them clean away.

We thought that they would come up
    like bubbles, these children,
    finding the light innately,
    by their very beings,
    so full of fire and oxygen.

Before,
    on that other shore
    that I can't remember now,
    there seemed a lack, a missingness
    that I was desperate to fill,
    but it has become an open wound
    of terrible love;
    one that never will heal,
    not now,

The Ways in Which We Are Like Birds

. . .

AND THINGS WILL NEVER BE as they were,
    for our hearts
    are walking around outside of us.
    We are no longer ourselves,

AND THIS IS why I think of these trucks,
    uncoupling,
    as I lie next to you
    in the black night,
    our daughter next to me on the bed,
    our son crying out in the other room.

Raye

I HAD EXPECTED to be full
    but there was this looming void
    and you at the edge of the screen,
    clinging on, the size of a lentil.
    You took root for a few weeks,
    but we never saw your heart beating;
    and the first time we looked,
    you had already left.

(RAY; a light shaft thrown across the floor,
    the luminous body from where the light streams.)

I THINK of you as a spirit;
    whispering at my ear,
    as a spark of light,
    an acorn of promise,

I THINK of you as a beginning
    that has not ended;
    a thought not fully realised.

YOU HAD NOT BEEN FULLY SKETCHED out,
    not on this earth at least.
    (Perhaps it could not hold you,
    that's what I tell myself.)

            . . .

AND SO, you are a comma,
    a seam between this life
    and the light which comes after.

Animae

> You were born in
> a flash of blood and pain.
> The children crept down
> from their beds to meet you,
> but then my heart raced
> and they sent us away.

'It wasn't supposed to go like this,'
> I said to the doctor, 'she's my fourth,
> it was meant to be fine,' as if
> my words could make it so.

I wasn't myself but muddled, frantic,
> staring out of the window,
> at the trees swaying noiselessly through the glass.
> I lay there looking at you side on,
> too scared to love you fully.

I looked up your name
> there on the blue-grey hospital bed,
> that close compartment of fear.

'Animae: a current of air, wind, breath,
> the vital principal, life, soul.'

Then I remembered that

you had been with me for years,
a pearl formed in the darkness of the ocean,
a dream that I couldn't ignore.

I KNEW that you would be okay,
    because your name had told me so.

THE DAYS and the infection slowly passed,
    and they let us out again,
    among the rush of the trees,
    the shock of new snow in the air.

There We Were (from *Paper Birds*)

There we were,
> walking among the greyhounds and labradors,
> their owners flinging tennis balls for them,
> and I thought none of this has the meaning for you that it does for me.
> For none of you it is the most beautiful, crisp March day that you wanted,
> as you walked with your mother.
> For none of you children, walking in a line of four or five,
> taking up the whole path, crunching on your Easter chocolate,
> does it weigh as heavily as it does now, for me.
> None of you post Easter lunchers, who walk heavily,
> having gorged on lamb or chicken or duck,
> with apple pie, coffee, and chocolate.
> You will forget this Sunday because it is just as any other,
> but to me, it feels almost holy,
> because it is the weight of a memory being laid down.
> It is the star of a day, the jewel of one that I will come back to,
> that I will revisit in my dreams and in my stories.
> that I will remember when I remember you, Mum.

SONG

FROM VOICE AT THE WINDOW, ONE HUNDRED POEMS OF GRATITUDE WRITTEN DURING LOCKDOWN, 2020

Gratitude #6

EVEN THOUGH IT IS COLD,
    I am thankful
    for the warmth of the sun
    on my back
    as I stand in the school field,
    watching my daughter play football.
    And this thought
    comes back to mind,
    a thought that has been thought
    over eons, by millions of us.
    That it is no small miracle
    that the sun is neither too hot
    nor too cold to sustain us,
    that our small earth hangs
    at just the right point in space to

receive all of its life-giving goodness.
That any change, however slight,
in temperature,
in degree of tilt,
in air composition
would have sent us
spinning off into space,
would have snatched life,
and all of these
infinite possibilities away.

02.03.20

Gratitude #7

Knowing that you will be writing about
    gratitude sets your brain off
    on a different track
    from the moment you wake.
    You look for the good things, not the bad,
    and you roam through the day, taking notes.
    You can pick almost-words, now,
    from Annie's song; 'dabum,' 'fsssh,' 'light.'
    You hear the throaty call of a crow in the sunshine.
    You delight in the taste of a hazelnut latte with velvet foam,
    from that independent café; the best you've tasted anywhere.
    You wander in the sun with your husband and father-in-law,
    talking of dreams and future things.
    Later, your lovely Mum comes around
    to do the dishes and play with Annie,
    while you sit at your desk and write for one more hour,
    finding another character who is opening up before you
    and it delights your soul and your senses,
    and you think,
    I hope this gets somewhere
    because I think I have something to say.

03.03.20

Gratitude #19

I wake this morning and hear the soft coo
of the wood pigeon and hear the blackbirds sing.
The earth is warming up and it feels we should be
breathing a sigh of relief now that we have made it through winter.
Instead, the virus of fear is spreading, faster, even, than the virus itself.
But the earth knows nothing of this; it is readying itself for growth,
for spring, for summer, for life, and it is 'tutto andra bene'
that the Italians are singing from their windows; 'All will be well'.

15.03.20

Gratitude #25

Thankful for this house today,
>   the one that has guided us from one life into the next.
>   Last time we moved, we were young and
>   felt that everything was still before us.
>   And now, six and a half years later, I feel old.
>   My face has changed, and my heart has too.
>   It was here, in this old house that we sat down,
>   eight weeks after moving, six weeks after Benjamin arrived,
>   with our sorrows, with broken hearts for our daughter,
>   newly diagnosed with Type 1 diabetes.
>   It was here that our life was undone
>   and built up again from scratch.
>   It was here that I made two books,
>   and watched my children grow
>   into these strange and beautiful beings,
>   utterly set apart from me, completely their own.
>   It is here that I have laughed many times and cried many tears.
>   It is here that my husband has written his way
>   into the clouds in his Shedio.
>   So farewell dear house, old friend.
>   Thank you for being our shelter in the storm,
>   and our garden in the spring.

21.03.20

Gratitude #43

Sam and I take hold of Annie's hands, one each,
    and walk in the hot, hot sun down the lane.
    She is learning to walk and throws each leg out
    with unbent knees, and jerky, foreign movements.
    It is as hot as the hottest summer day,
    and we could all close our eyes and pretend that this isn't happening.
    It is quiet, and I long for the food to last for weeks,
    so I don't have to go out, to face the sad realities of life.
    We walk slowly down the dusty track to the bridge
    and look at the field of lambs on either side of the road.
    Annie points at them, in all their newness and whiteness.
    Sam says, 'Can we do this again, go for a walk, just us?'
    And I think it is magical how the simplest, the plainest of things
    are the things that they want to do again.
    I swear as parents we sometimes want to do
    more and more and more for our children,
    but maybe what they need is less and less and less.
    Until there is just us, standing by a field and talking,
    holding hands with our sweet girl,
    leading her back up the lane.

08.04.20

GRATITUDE #49

THE A49, normally so full
    of fight or flight,
    is now a pale empty ribbon
    glinting in the sunlight.
    Our lives, once so jam-packed
    that there was no time to think,
    have been emptied out too.

AND WHAT DOES it feel like now?
    Stripped back and bare, empty but still full.

PERHAPS WE ARE LEARNING AGAIN,
    how to be at peace,
    how to pace ourselves,
    how to conserve our strength,
    how to keep going,
    one day at a time.

14.04.20

Gratitude #52

Learning today from the wisdom of the trees.
  There is a young tree standing on its own, in a clearing,
  perfectly symmetrical because it has the space
  to expand in any way it wants to.
  I wonder what can grow in us now that
  the land had been cleared around us.
  The second is a group of branches, gathered low at the stem.
  They sway in the wind, and if they couldn't move, they would crack.
  Their strength is in their ability to bend and swerve, to flex and shift.
  I wonder if our roots are being strengthened
  as we come around to this new way of being.
  The third tree was felled by a storm, hollowed out at its core,
  and from its carcass new growth shoots up.
  Not a thin shoot, but a strong new branch with flawless, youthful bark,
  and I wonder what will come from the carcass of this year?
  Something stronger, resilient, a vivid shoot of green?

17.04.20

Gratitude #57

I turn to see the bright field
    at dusk,
    in the inky blue of bedtime,
    and then first thing
    in the morning,
    where it glows against the
    warming sky like a beacon
    or a flash of hope.

It is a new day.

22.04.20

Gratitude #59

Dear birds,
    please be our healers,
    our message bringers,
    our sweet talkers.
    Whether we be city dwellers
    or country folk,
    you birds are the only ones
    who can visit us all.
    Whether we have lost our best friend,
    or are tethered to our home,
    whether we are lonely or overcrowded,
    may your gentle 'per-wit,'
    your 'chee-chee,'
    your slow 'coo-coo'
    be a balm to our souls.
    May we sleep like birds of the air
    who know they have a nest.
    May we wake in the morning
    like sparrows who know
    that they are cared for.
    And wherever we are,
    may we find an open window
    and listen.

24.04.20

GRATITUDE #70

FOR THE GENTLE peep peep
    of the train that passes
    at the back of the house.
    It makes me feel connected
    in all this aloneness.
    At night, its lit-up windows
    are a streamer of light
    across the darkness.
    For the 'baas' of the sheep
    in the field down the hill
    that make me feel grounded
    in all this aloneness,
    pinned to the earth.
    For the crows calling,
    for the warm wind
    that rustles the leaves, and says 'Ssh,'
    still yourself, all will be well.
    For all the normal, glorious things
    that happen each day
    and go on happening.

05.05.20

Gratitude #71

The full moon, glowing at dusk,
    and the audacious song thrush
    calling out from his tree,
    so small, but yet so loud!
    He calls, repeats,
    waits and calls again.
    It makes me wonder how
    loud our songs are heard
    and how far they spread
    beyond our knowing.

06.05.20

GRATITUDE #77

Was it the high track along the ridgeback,
    not another human in sight?
    Was it the birds circling as we walked,
    calling and swooping down, as if looking for carrion?
    Was it the clouds lighting up the shapes of these hills
    that we know and love, that we now call our home?
    Or the wind lifting our hair away from our faces,
    the children running ahead of us, as wild as ever,
    Annie chatting into the wind?
    Who can say what I am most thankful for,
    what is the most important, or what I will remember from this day?
    But this much I know; I've always loved this hill,
    the way it sets one path before you,
    and says choose this, there is no other way,
    just this one will take you there.

12.05.20

Gratitude #82

Today I wake to the sound of birdsong.
    It is a cloak of joy around me
    and I remember how Annie
    is always happy when she wakes.
    It reminds me to be the same.
    We have a coffee in the garden
    while the children play.
    We make roast chicken for lunch
    with lemon, garlic and thyme.
    It is one of those days
    where the day is sliced in two,
    where you don't understand
    how this is going to go away,
    or how we will ever get through this,
    where you miss your parents,
    your family, your friends.
    But at the same time, you realise
    that finding the little things
    and naming them
    will hold you up from day to day.

17.05.20

A Note to the Creatives

A note to all the creatives
    who cannot hear their own thoughts.
    Who cannot produce work
    because they cannot hear,
    who cannot hear because
    there is no time that is not
    filled to the brim with voices.
    I want to say, and I want it to be true
    that your work is not lost,
    that your poems are not
    escaping through your fingers,
    running away from you.
    I have said that before,
    but it is different this time,
    because all of us are trying
    to make sense of this,
    in this time where we have
    all the time and no time.
    Those words will come back at the right time
    if you have eyes that are open,
    if you have ears for hearing,
    if you are willing to go a little slower
    than you normally would have.

Gratitude #85

Inside it is messy,
    and there are so many people
    living all of their hours in this space
    that it is hard to keep on top of everything.

I step outside
    and the sky is huge and bare,
    the light on the hills is just right,
    and the cool breeze on my skin
    is like a cup of cold water to the soul.

I can hear a field full of sheep calling
    and the gentle strains of a piano
    from behind a closed door.
    There is all the time in the world,
    it seems, all the space in the world.

20.05.20

GRATITUDE #87

TODAY HAS SLIPPED
    through my fingers, somehow.
    It has got away from me before
    I have had a chance to do
    anything useful with it.
    How many days are like this now?
    The wind whips the long grass
    into a fury in the field.
    The ash tree shakes itself
    mournfully outside the window.
    See how nature itself is fast and slow,
    yet we do not count the grass
    more worthy than the tree?
    Going fast is not everything.
    And so today is everything
    and nothing,
    just as every other day is.

22.05.20

Gratitude #92

It seems so much like all of this
    is about rest:
    the being in one place,
    the undoing of all that is normal.

I stubbornly plough on with work
    while Annie naps,
    diving desperately down for jewels,
    like a starving kingfisher.

Later, she drinks her milk
    in the hammock,
    and I listen to the others
    shrieking with delight, a way off.
    I realise I must claim this minute,
    this stillness,
    because otherwise it will be gone.

And after everything, the silver birches
    are all soft and forgiveness and grace,
    each day of this unassuming year.

27.05.20

Gratitude #95

Even though he is now six,
    he still has a little heart inside of him,
    and in the scorching sun we get out planks of wood
    to make a ramp down the steps for his hot wheels.
    He shows his baby sister the joy of cars,
    and she squeals with delight as she watches them go
    and then puts one on the track herself.
    When he was at preschool,
    I would buy him a new car every few weeks,
    in return for good behaviour at the supermarket.
    It was my love letter to him in metal and paint,
    and even now, big boy, little boy,
    he pulls out his drawer, crammed full of cars,
    and searches among them for the one he is looking for,
    turns it around in his hands,
    says, 'This is my best, he's the fastest'.

30.05.20

Gratitude #106

Stumbling, bleary-eyed
    into the lounge at 6.40am,
    I see the pink-red glow of the horizon,
    and these birds, high, high up,
    migrating south.

We saw others last night at dusk,
    and now, this morning, scores more.
    It is overwhelming
    that they all know what to do,
    without the need for words,
    when here we all are;
    all of our words
    and not a way of escaping,
    all of our intelligence and civilisation
    and we just don't know what to do.

But they journey on in certainty,
    and each time I see them,
    I am filled with questions like;
    'How do they know where to go?'
    and 'What do they do if they get lost?'
    The first year in a new house
    is one of surprises, and this,
    the path of migration,
    against the rose-glow of the morning
    is the biggest gift.

. . .

28.09.20

Gratitude #113

The slightly bedraggled Acer
    stopped me in my tracks today.
    It hasn't really had a home
    since we moved
    and has been moved about in its pot
    from place to place.
    But today it shone in autumn glory,
    red, orange, green: so small, so beautiful.
    And I thought, What if this is its only job this year,
    its proudest moment?
    What if this is what it is here for?
    this shining, silvery joy,
    this unashamed basking in the sunlight,
    this glorying in the self?
    And then I thought,
    Maybe I can learn
    a thing or two
    from this little tree.

5.10.20

Gratitude #115

Being with one as young as this
    makes everything feel new.
    Even a walk down the lane
    when there is a break
    in the clouds
    has everything we need for joy:
    dandelions, baa baas,
    choo-choos, muddy puddles,
    a plane in the sky, lorries.

It's her wisdom
    that I am thankful for today;
    See how she is
    overwhelmed
    with delight
    at this life.

07.10.20

Gratitude #120

It rains all day,
    and then,
    after the kids eat,
    we wander down the lane
    where the puddles
    are full to the brim,
    and the sky is pink
    and lit from within.

I had a headache
    but it disappeared.
    The children were fighting
    but they start to run instead.
    This is what we need.

The sky is cold,
    and it shocks us
    out of ourselves.

12.10.20

GRATITUDE #130

FOR THE BRIGHT, bright colours of autumn,
    for the salmon who have travelled
    thousands of miles to get back here, to their river,
    and now we wait, and now we see them
    leap, clear of the water,
    heading upstream, against all odds.

23.10.20

Gratitude #133

It is only when we are walking one step ahead of the other
    on these coarse, grassy banks that we feel ourselves.
    Only when we pass through bog and freezing stream,
    down a sheep track and up the narrow valley, up, up to the top,
    where everything is kissed with an October glow,
    with a chill in the air, that we feel at home.
    The bracken has turned brittle and covers the backs of these old hills,
    with its rust, making them soft on the eye, the heart.

26.10.20

Gratitude #147

I AM STILL SEARCHING for things to hold on to,
 for the jewels in the day, as these days get shorter and more uncertain.
 Today, the air is mild, and we take the children to town for haircuts.
 Afterwards, we go down to the cafe by the river,
 where five geese beat their wings down against the water,
 pushing them uncannily aloft.
 They are so close that we can hear their wings move,
 as their large and soft bodies take slow flight down the river.
 This town has never been more lovely,
 bathed in yellow and orange,
 with splashes of red
 along the banks of the Severn.
 I breathe in the mild autumn air,
 and turn back to the children,
 cutting three cakes six ways,
 while they sip babycinos with teaspoons.

30.10.20

Gratitude #154

The trees and the light
>here will never get old.

The late sun
>falls
>through the yellowing
>leaves
>like hope.

And hope, like the sun,
>has been quietly waiting,

For a crack in the clouds,
>a way through the leaves,

To bring its gold.

06.11.20

Gratitude #166

The way she sits there,
    in deep concentration,
    drawing a line upon each nail
    in felt tip.

And later, when she is in the bath
    babbling away to herself,
    and I am just watching her,
    I realise that I still can't quite
    believe that she's here with us.

For so many years I waited for her,
    and now she is here,
    taking up the whole of each day
    with her chatter and mess and beauty.

19.11.20

Gratitude #181

I WEAR gratitude like a cloak
    so the grey can't get in.
    I have been looking to the horizon,
    waiting for this storm to pass,
    but all I can hear
    is the stifling sound
    of the buffeting wind,
    the whipping fury of it
    spinning through strangers' lives,
    dispossessing them.

So I READY myself
    in the eye of the storm,
    arming myself against its desolation
    with a list of delights;
    my daughter sings a song today,
    a crocus blooms,
    the new lambs cry out
    and the sun is warm on my face
    as I go running with my son.

I WILL LOSE myself in these incidentals
    until the storm has passed,
    almost as if I were concentrating
    on the shape of a flower,
    or something else so beautiful and small,
    until the tears stopped coming.

            . . .

15.02.21

PREENING

Sometimes

S<small>OMETIMES THERE IS SO</small> much noise around you,
    that you can't even feel the stillness.
    Sometimes you bring with you so much talking
    that you have lost all sense of quiet.

S<small>O</small>, you sit at the stream,
    and tell the children to play football
    further up the valley.
    It takes a while, but you wait
    until all you can hear
    is the ripple of the water,
    running in rivulets,
    falling into pools.

Sometimes it Feels **Impossible**

Like tonight,
    when Sam tried to jump through the swing
    and landed on his shoulder,
    and the red dots went down his arm.
    Everything creative scuttled away then;
    those shy creatures, who had come out
    and begun to dwell with us
    bolted at the first sign of stress like furtive deer.
    Something in him is always asking to be the best,
    the strongest, the fastest,
    and his body bears the blows of his bad choices.
    How can we look after these souls that are
    entrusted to us, but so full of wispy danger?
    They make bad choices all the time,
    and we have no choice but to stand back
    and let it happen.

Ash

We are so high up here,
    that the ash seems almost at eye level.
    The wood pigeons hinge their wings on the air,
    and I can almost taste their effort
    as they heave their fat bodies along.
    They sing at night, pulling dusk up around us
    like a sleeping bag,
    lulling themselves to sleep with song.

Seed Pods

I LOOK DOWN at my sleeve
    and see a handful of seed pods
    clinging there.
    This is their whole reason for being,
    I realise;
    holding on,
    and letting themselves be carried
    somewhere new.

From April 2022

Mouthful

The blue tits sing
    such a complicated song.
    It trills and peaks in the waning light
    on this cold April day,
    it clicks and burrs
    like the tuning of a radio.

They race overhead
    with this song quick in their mouths,
    so full of its own lilt and tilt,
    full as a mouthful of worms.

Curled Like a Cat

I think of her curled like a cat,
    the needle drawing fluid from her spine.
    They told us she had vomited,
    and handed back her dirty baby grow,
    when they brought her back to us,
    quiet with surprise.
    They kept telling us about her numbers,
    but I was dazed and didn't understand.
    We just wanted her bare and untarnished,
    like it should be on day one.

Like a Whip

There are times when we think
    we can't hold this together,
    all this want and need.
    There are only two of us and four of them,
    pulling us this way and that.
    We wonder if he should give up
    Sunday league so we can have a day to rest,
    but then I watch him on the pitch,
    dancing on the ball,
    see the way he strikes like a whip;
    his pointed toe like a ballerina's,
    in that curious combination of precision and drive.
    All the while he is keen, alert, hungry,
    and I think, how could we take that away from him?

UKRAINE

I just watched a tank drive over a civilian car
    on someone's Instagram profile.
    It made me sick to the stomach, to watch
    the extinction of life on the screen of my iPhone;
    the way the car stopped, so abruptly,
    as if its driver knew what was coming.
    What can I do, so far away,
    cowering in fear of the news,
    but also scrolling my screen for updates?
    What can I do for those mothers and children,
    fleeing along bombed corridors,
    their hands in their pockets,
    their whole lives in their backpacks,
    their cities flattened behind them?

Magnolia

These past few weeks,
    the sight of the magnolia
    coming into bloom
    at the end of the road
    has been a balm,
    a kiss of life on a cold day.

But the white blooms
    are already turning to brown
    and it breaks my heart a little.

So beautiful, here, and then gone.

Magnolia, I have always loved you,
    heralder of spring.

Piano

When you play,
    and the clear notes
    come filtering through
    the kitchen
    to the lounge,
    she stops playing
    and looks up,
    drawn by the sound
    of something
    that she must go after.

She puts down her car
    and follows.
    And, finding you,
    she sits down and plays too,
    trying to make those same sounds
    with her own hands.

Swallow

The tree has swallowed bricks and stones in his slow embrace of years,
    has grown through the wall and pulled them all along with him.

He sewed them into himself with his year-long strides,
    tucking his problems under his wing.

And in the end, all of the troubles were hidden in his kind embrace, his forgetting,
    and in the end, he stands much mightier than they.

Half Marathon

It looked as if she was holding back
    to begin with,
    but then she pushed through
    and by lap four, she was flying.
    Afterwards she said 'I feel sick'
    and the sweat glistened on her skin.

There is hidden scaffolding
    behind her running;
    a bumbag full of jelly babies,
    an asterisk on her bib,
    the Dexcom,
    the phone in her pocket.

Someone said to us a long time ago
    that she would grow far and wide
    with support, just like ivy does.

So it is up to me to be invisible
    so she can be normal,
    be a pancreas on the sidelines;
    · in car parks and at night times.
    And I take that job with joy
    so she can stay carefree
    a little longer.

        · · ·

NOTE: *My daughter has Type 1 diabetes and this poem speaks about the support behind the scenes.*

Sleep

'Can you look after me?'
    she says, 'I want to go to sleep,'
    and I stroke her bare feet
    until she breathes heavily
    next to me in her car seat;
    her head heavy, her hair tangled.
    We have travelled hundreds
    of miles this weekend,
    and she is young enough
    to believe that I am home,
    wherever we are,
    and what joy, little one,
    it is to be your anchor.

Hope

THE THING about springtime
    is that it can never disappoint you;
    all of its bunched-up blossoms
    waiting in the wings
    for their time to unfurl,
    like a row of ballerinas.

SPRING'S SONG IS HOPE, but also waiting,
    and being hope-filled in the waiting,
    knowing that what came before
    will come again.

I SEE THE FIELDS, half-yellow,
    the Mexican orange buds loosening,
    the alliums shooting skyward,
    all of them poised for their time to bloom.

At Whixall Moss

We walk out to a place
    that feels miles from anywhere,
    where birds score the sky with their flight,
    and drown us out with their calls.
    The sun beats down on us
    as we search for snakes,
    all of us quiet under these skies
    that do not belong to us.
    Sam walks carefully up and down,
    scanning the ground for movement.
    'I saw a tail,' he says, his eyes brightening,
    and we all look then,
    beneath the bracken,
    near to the water,
    but it does not come for us.

Alliums

Slim sentinels along the fence,
    they have pushed up through colder days,
    and now stand ready.

Slowly, slowly, they come into being,
    purple tassels peeping.
    Each day I watch for them to burst open.

Ridge Line

Sometimes
>I can't remember why I write.
>My heart is full of wishful thinking
>and my inbox is full of noise.

I am waiting.

At these times,
>I wash up often,
>listening to the
>thread of my thoughts,
>running on.
>I stand outside with cups of tea.
>I crave silence.

It feels like I am heading
>for one of those moments,
>walking along a ridge line,
>or coming to a fork on the road.

It feels like I must
>put everything down
>and listen.

I know I must ask,

'Is this still the right thing?
Should I be putting this down
and doing something else?'

AND THEN, fortified,
    or reminded, I will bury myself
    in my words again,
    trusting that they carry a small flame,
    will mean something to someone.

Soak

I sat and leaned back into the sun.
    I breathed sun-filled breaths,
    and tried to remember winter.

I heard the peep peep of a train pass,
    and the whirr of lorries on the road behind me,
    but I was not in their rushing.

I smelled the beginning scents of spring,
    breathed them into the top of my lungs
    and held them there.

I sat and let the whole world soak into me,
    just for a moment,
    until my daughter called my name.

Dreamer's Workshop

Sometimes it takes having my feet
    pulled out from under me to stop.
    I woke with nausea
    which settled only when I lay down,
    so I did, and daydreamed like I did
    in the days before there were children.
    I picture colour schemes,
    and dream of changing things
    in the children's bedrooms
    until they are all just right,
    and we all fall perfectly into place
    in our origami house.
    Nothing is ever perfect though,
    and nothing is really ever finished either,
    because life is growing, changing, shifting
    and nothing stays the same.
    So, I will wait in the in-between,
    and make my life in the half-finished;
    a dreamer's workshop,
    where everything is still possible.

Mexican Wave

The blooms spread across the field
    like a Mexican wave.
    Even now, from up here,
    they are a wild shock of yellow.
    They glow at dusk,
    drawing me to the window
    with their brilliance.

Bluebell

We pull into the driveway at dusk
    where the scent of bluebells is heavy on the air,
    reminding me that life is sweet,
    that its scent is long lasting
    and fragrant too.

After everything
    when the day is done,
    and all other distractions have gone,
    it fills the night with itself,
    says, 'See? I told you so.'

Taken from *Lent Poems*

Cleanse

I think of washing something
    so hot and so thoroughly
    that it comes out like new.
    I think of the white lambs
    down the lane again,
    untarnished by this muddy life,
    (except for their bony knees,
    for they must kneel to find
    their mother's milk).
    And just like this,
    life has a way of sullying, doesn't it?
    Of tiring, dirtying, and distracting us,
    when all we really want
    is to come out of the wash like new,
    pure of heart,
    like the lambs,
    untired of this life,
    gambolling their way
    through the days.

See

'My life is the light
    that pierces the world's darkness,'
    he said,
    as he spat on the ground.
    He knelt to scoop up a handful
    of spittle and mud
    and rubbed it in his palm to make a paste.
    He smeared it gently on the man's eyes.
    'Blind from birth,'
    we whispered between ourselves,
    'His eyes didn't even form in the womb.'
    But he went to wash in the pool of Siloam,
    like Jesus said to,
    and as he blinked away the water
    from his eyes, there was colour,
    there was light for the first time.
    And then, a piercing shout,
    'I can see!'
    And he wept,
    because it was impossible.
    And here we were
    in the presence of the impossible.
    He waded, trembling, back towards us,
    marvelling in the light,
    the trees, the clouds,
    seeing for the first time,
    the faces of the ones he loved,
    seeing the one who pierced his darkness:
    Jesus.
    We spit for disrespect, for disgust,

and here he was,
bringing eyes back to life,
healing and restoring
with mud and spittle,
mixing earth and heaven
in the palm of his hand.

Walk

To walk is the simple act
    of putting one foot in front
    of another,
    even if you are not sure
    where you are going,
    and the truth is
    that you are not alone,
    but there is another
    who walks
    alongside,
    or even carrying.

Follow

Follow,
    not as the sheep follows,
    unthinking and mindless.
    Follow rather as a listener
    on foot in a vast and lonely hill country,
    paying attention only
    to the placing of the feet,
    one in front of the other,
    on the soft and craggy ground,
    listening to the small voice that speaks,
    that says, this way, this way,
    call it intuition or God.
    Or follow as the fox,
    who tracks by staying alert,
    ready to change course at once,
    his nose twitching
    with the strange scent
    on the air.

Promise

THE LITTLE TREE,
    (I don't even know its name)
    knows the promise.
    Its buds loosen,
    ready to bloom with pops of colour
    because it holds within its DNA
    the promise of spring.
    Though it tarries, wait for it.

AND I WONDER what we carry
    to show that spring is coming,
    to show that the promise of heaven
    is held in the very fibre of our being?

Room

He said to wait, and so we waited.
    For what? For him again.
    For the light to come back
    and show us what to do next,
    and how to live.
    And so we waited,
    eleven of us,
    in the cramped room,
    filled with a thin kind of emptiness –
    what were we to do now?

And then it came,
    the roaring wind,
    tearing us up from the inside.
    And then it came,
    the holy fire;
    burning the sadness away,
    filling the empty rooms
    of ourselves
    with a new way of living.

For Sarah

I TOO, have walked home
    faster than normal,
    with a raised heartbeat
    and the sound of my own footsteps
    loud in my ears.
    I too, have run back to the parked car,
    and only felt safe
    when I closed the door
    and pulled away.
    I have been twitchy
    and looked over my shoulder
    when someone was coming up behind me
    and jumped when I saw them so close.
    I have wished myself invisible,
    have wished also that this body
    had been made a little stronger.
    Two days after International Women's Day,
    where we said we could do anything,
    we realise too
    that she is all of us
    and that any one of us could be her.

Keep Watch

Could you imagine being fully God
    and fully man, asking your friends
    to stay a while with you,
    to keep watch with you,
    even though you knew
    they would fail, and even though
    you knew you would have to walk alone
    the path that was laid out before you?
    A death sentence that would unleash
    freedom in its wake.
    Spinner of stars,
    watcher in the dark,
    you wondered if your father
    could not have found another way.
    But his way was you, beloved son,
    diving into the heart of death
    to break its power from within.
    The one who flipped the switch
    from dark to light.
    Underpinner, the one in whom
    all of this hangs together -
    the rhythms and reasons of this planet,
    the migrations and moons,
    all the tides of time,
    and all the souls
    who come and go.
    But still your friends
    couldn't keep watch with you,
    they let you down,

king of the universe,
trembling in the garden.

Sacrifice

These gifts
    we hold lightly,
    their warp and weft,
    their stretch and sway
    as they wend their way
    through our lives,
    threading them with
    just a touch
    of heaven's fire.
    We live through them,
    and through them
    make sense of this world.
    We see you, God,
    we even draw you,
    in green and grace,
    in white and gold,
    in ink and pencil,
    because we are trying,
    always,
    to make sense of this.
    Here is the sacrifice:
    of time and devotion,
    instead of promotion
    and the sensible way.
    Here instead,
    a different way of living:
    a fractured and colourful life,
    an imperfect offering
    on an outstretched palm.
    So may this seed grow,

shooting and green,
vivid and life giving,
until it reaches
all the fullness
it was made for.

Cross

A SINGLE SEED lay down in the soil,
    and from it sprang life,
    a tree, reaching to the heavens.
    A single tree, cut down,
    fashioned into planks
    and then a cross
    bearing the weight
    of the blameless King,
    a man, who was a tree of life himself,
    who walked the path into death
    and then out the other side,
    so that his death, his planting,
    would reap blessing
    for generation
    after generation;
    a tree of life,
    his branches spreading wide,
    his roots reaching deep
    for all who come.
    And every drop of life from him,
    another seed,
    and every breath of life from him,
    a seed bearer.

Cloths

Their very presence speaks
    to what is no longer there;
    the way that they fall, or are folded.
    There is the dance of life about them;
    the way they move themselves aside,
    lift themselves up, to let Life take its first breath.

Hidden

YOU WERE HIDDEN
    in death, in grave clothes,
    waiting for the right time
    to take your first breath
    of rebirth.
    And now I am hidden in you,
    safe as houses,
    where moth and rust
    cannot break in and destroy,
    because all my treasure is in you
    and you are all my treasure.

Darkness

I SEE God bowed and brooding,
    his arms falling around his dear earth,
    after cruel jeers
    condemned his son to death.
    Doubled up with grief,
    he came close to the jagged earth,
    his arms around, almost touching.
    And it reminds me of this year;
    of all the loneliness,
    the people in their boxes,
    staying safe by staying alone.
    Perhaps God is bent
    and broken by our grief,
    by our struggles too?
    Perhaps he comes close
    when the darkness is too dark
    to see by?

WAIT

THE TWO MEN
 on the road to Emmaus
 had forgotten how to wait;
 they had moved on too quickly
 to despair;
 'We had hoped he
 was the one who was going to
 redeem Israel,' they said.
 They had already given up hope,
 had tossed it by the wayside,
 in favour of despair.
 Perhaps it comes quicker,
 is easier to hold.
 But there is strength in waiting,
 in hearing a promise
 and planting it deep in your heart.
 There were those who lived like this,
 staring down old age and infertility
 with God's promise,
 believing for something
 as wild and outlandish as this:
 a child from a lifeless womb,
 a screaming mass of bone and flesh,
 but it came, it came,
 and like Abraham,
 we must learn to live our lives this way;
 waiting for the third day,
 holding on to hope,
 and the words that have been spoken,

no matter how barren or broken
things seem.
The story isn't over yet,
though it tarries, wait for it.

Dawn

IT STARTS off
    as the slightest lightening
    in the colourless dark,
    almost imperceptible at first
    and then, a little bolder,
    and soon enough
    the rose-gold glow
    colours the sky
    from east to west.
    It starts out so small:
    just a scratch of light
    against the darkness,
    but you know the power
    of the sun,
    and you keep watching
    as the dark
    dissolves
    into light.

FLIGHT

I am Woman

I AM WOMAN.
    I don't need to wait for death
    to be scattered to the wind;
    parts of me are already everywhere.

MY TEARS HAVE GONE DOWN the drain,
    and my unborn baby slipped out of me,
    when I so wanted him or her,
    whoever they were.

FOUR TIMES, an organ of mine
    has been tied up and disposed of,
    in an NHS plastic bag,

so, you see -
I am neither here nor there.

BROKEN in two each time I birthed,
    and now I am many, and all my hearts
    go walking around outside of me.

GHOST WOMAN -
    half-awake and half-myself;
    the drag of anxiety has eaten me alive.

AND I, half-seeing, half-living,
    can't remember who I am anymore.

HALF-DEAD BECAUSE THEY ARE ALIVE,
    tripping over myself
    to make sure they are okay.

Love

Love is just love, isn't it?
    I mean it just goes on and on,
    a river making its way
    to the sea, no explanation for its course,
    except that it chooses the easiest way,
    the way of least resistance,
    and sometimes that means
    flooding fields, sometimes
    crashing into buildings.

I know not where my love will run,
    all I know is that I let it go,
    stream to the river,
    river to the sea.

On Hearing

On hearing that there have been 100,000 deaths,

I am gutted like a fish,
    hollowed out like an empty shell,

or else I am that
    homeless spirit,
    set free, and wandering -

wondering how we got here.

Was it our government? Chance?
    The nature of our nation;
    small, tight knit, old, multicultural?

The biggest thing
    we have to learn at home school today is

How do we stay alive?
    and how do we keep those we love alive?

but also - how do we steady ourselves
    against this tsunami of loss?

. . .

The one thing I know is
 to be quiet and look.

See how the thin stalk of a snowdrop
 pushes up through the ground,
 its paper-frail head bowed
 in prayer, or regret?

See how the birds
 start the day at 5am,
 with joy their first thought,
 the dawn song in their mouths?

So may our silent worries,
 our black and sinking hearts
 return us to the earth,
 where we might hold tight to life,
 to mud and grass miracles,
 to the littlest,
 most beautiful things,

that keep us tethered,
 yet also keep us afloat.

Clearing, Spring

'Leave a little wilderness at the edge,'
    a quiet voice says,
    as I wrestle the garden into submission.
    Brambles tear my flesh as I rip them up,
    the whole force of my body, pivot and crane.

This is the modern way;
    no mess or clutter,
    no question unanswered.
    Edges, neatly defined.
    But if we all tidied ourselves like this,
    there would be nowhere to travel on to -
    no room for wondering, no thread left to follow.

'Leave a little wilderness at the edge of yourself,'
    the voice says again,
    'And walk there sometimes, and look into it;
    towards all the questions you haven't thought of yet,
    and all the unknowings of your life.
    And see then, the great mystery;
    that closure is never an option,
    but dwelling with, and letting be
    is the better way.'

And so, I put down my tools,
    and think of the quiet gift of the bramble,

rambling along at the edge of things,
speaking of all I don't yet know,
putting me in my place again,
with its gifts of thorn and fruit.

Bones

I know what it is to mourn a friendship,
    a seismic shift that leaves nothing unaltered.

You can't see the whole of it,
    only this part now, where it hurts.

It undoes and remakes you,
    like any common tragedy,

and you are knocked back
    to the bare bones of yourself.

But you will stand
    and become the very
    you-ness of you again,

because you are a force
    that cannot be stopped,
    no matter how they come and go.

Mother

There's a sheep in the field
    at the end of the lane.
    She hasn't moved all day.

This morning
    there was a dirty lump
    on the ground beside her,
    showing up against the snow.

The farmer must have taken it away
    when he brought food, later on.

I see myself in her,
    the way she stares ahead motionless,
    while the others mill around her.

She waits for something to be undone,
    for something to be different,
    and stands in quiet shock
    at what is.

She can't move on from it,
    so she waits quietly,
    her gaze fixed ahead,

where that dirty lump of hers
once breathed and came running.

Yearlet

Climbing out of the week's mire,
    we cling to Yearlet's mane,
    pulling ourselves up and up
    to the safety of its smooth flanks.

We don't know the way,
    but must get there anyway.

Every step is a silence,
    a pilgrimage,
    a need.

Half-way there,
    we turn to see how far we've come
    and the wind cools the sweat against our skin.

It feels like coming up for air.

We look for home,
    look for our favourite hills
    and name them;
    Ragleth, Caradoc, Lawley, Wrekin.

By finding where we are,

we find ourselves.
We place ourselves again
on the map of our lives -
and descend,
re-found,
re-oriented.

Having a Hard Time

I just need ten minutes
to myself, I say.
I can't even hear myself think
these days,
can't even finish a sentence.
And so, I go outside
and lean into the wind,
my mouth an o,
my howl lost in the
crashing fury
upon the back
of this sad hill.
I stand there,
breathing the world in,
letting it go.

Maple

The maple has this way
    of making itself new every year.

No matter how old or gnarled it gets,
    it unfurls this squeaky newness each spring;
    Its sticky, clean leaves, like a frog's pads,
    or the hot clammy grasp of a new-born.

And it leaves me thinking
    I would like to have
    some part of myself reborn,
    made completely new each year.

I think of my tired eyes,
    and my spent body,
    but also, those poems and books
    waiting to come into being.

Perhaps they will be my newness,
    each poem, an unfurling leaf?

And so, I begin to listen,
    to write myself into happiness,
    to set my thoughts in straight lines,

because even a little crafted thing
landing on the page,
can be a thing of beauty.

Sometimes

Sometimes
    there aren't the words
    to describe the relief you feel
    at the sight of beauty, of order.
    It is the quiet reassurance
    that beyond all of this
    rage and worry,
    the old Earth
    knows its rhythms.
    Its sunsets cast their pink beauty,
    its snow falls, and the damp
    lifts all the smells from the earth
    that are good,
    and life-bringing,
    and ancient and true.
    And every step reminds me
    that it will be okay,
    because I am part
    of this ancient living thing.
    It carries me and
    I am small in the world's arms,
    and although ravaged,
    it whispers to me,
    'I have got this.'

Things the Summer Teaches

That as soon as it is here,
  it is already thinking of leaving.
  I haven't even paused for thought,
  haven't truly felt the warmth of summer,
  and already it starts to spin away.
  Midsummer gets me every year.
  'Stay on and bloom,' I plead, 'don't leave.'

That the leaves will always fall,
  no matter how tightly
  I clutch summer to my chest.

That I can't stop this world from turning,
  however hard I dig my heels in.

That it won't rest for tragedy, heartbreak, or despair,
  but spins tirelessly on, drawing each day to itself,
  filling its spool with the thread of the everyday.

That my children will outrun me, even the littlest,
  that my job, after all of this, is just to let go.

That these four came to me like birds for the winter,
  and are preening their wings on the wire again,
  readying themselves for flight.

Rose

SEE how the rose that I hacked right back
    is budding again, already?
    Pushing out new buds from its tired old bark,
    getting back to the business of living again.

Unfurl

At last!
    Down the lane
    we find ourselves
    walking out of winter.
    The sun warms,
    the buds
    unfurl.

Speak, River-Sea

>It is the way the wood
>falls behind the houses,
>the ancient oaks
>crumbling to fine matter,
>surrendering themselves
>to the undoing of everything.

>And in front, it is the way the people
>turn themselves to the water,
>first thing in the morning,
>and last thing at night –
>as if it has all the answers.

They wait
>for its stillness
>to speak to them,
>its silky glide, a guide.

>The boy can't sleep
>because he loves this place so much,
>and doesn't want to say goodbye.

And still the people watch
>as the estuary slips over itself,
>and its currents whirl and eddy.

See how the water moves

upstream, filling, filling
and the sea pulls it down again,
drawing it in like breath?

Speak river-sea,
    we are listening.

Why Does It Take So Long?

Why does it take so long to be still,
    to learn names that are not our own,
    to listen as the dusk falls,
    the world around us softly glows,
    and all of life comes into being?

Even the smallest of birds
    make themselves known in the dusk
    like some indelible ink stain,
    some fluorescent prayer,
    a little cry.

And I wonder,
    why can't we be more like this?
    More at one with our speaking,
    our making,
    our luminescence?

Be bold, then,
    like the birds,
    singing in the dusk,
    because it is so pink and light.

ACKNOWLEDGMENTS

Thank you to everyone who has read any of my poems, whether in a book, on the website, or on my social media pages. I have had wonderful feedback for some of these poems as I have posted them over the years.

Posting a poem feels like a litmus test for its viability. Does it connect with the reader? Does it move them to tears? Does it speak to them? When the answer to any of these questions is yes, then I know the poem is true, and has worth because of that, regardless of any industry rejections I may have had for it. I felt that these poems were weighty little things and I wanted to put them out as a collection.

Some of the poems have been previously published in *There You Are,* as hand-lettered versions, and I wanted these to be available in a text only version too. Some were previously published in *Voice at the Window.* Many others have not been previously published. The first of these poems were written in 2006, before I had children, and the latest of them was written a few years ago. This collection feels like a dense, compacted slice of life; joys and sorrows from over the years, packed down to make rich compost.

Thanks go to Len and Cherry Howes, Hilary Thomas and Vicky Barnes for proofreading and offering editorial suggestions on the poems. I would also like to thank my online writers' group for their support and comradeship!

I hope that the poems in this book will lift and inspire

you to take a little more joy in who you are, and to sing a little louder at dusk.

Thanks so much for picking up this poetry book, I hope you enjoyed it. If you did, I would be hugely grateful for a review either at Amazon here: https://amzn.eu/d/2qpBBVd or at GoodReads here: https://www.goodreads.com/book/show/227801374-the-ways-in-which-we-are-like-birds

Every review helps another reader to find my books. If any of the poems have spoken to you, please reach out and let me know at elisabeth_pike@yahoo.co.uk – I love to hear from my readers!

If you want to stay in touch, please subscribe to my mailing list at Miners here, where I write about the creative life and share writing news: https://minersbyelisabethpike.substack.com/

You can also find me in these places:
    https://elisabethpike.co.uk
    https://www.instagram.com/elisabethpikewriter/
    https://www.facebook.com/elisabethpikewriter

Thanks so much for reading,

Elisabeth

www.ingramcontent.com/pod-product-compliance
Lightning Source LLC
Chambersburg PA
CBHW020533080526
44583CB00013B/839